Richard Lederer's

Literary
Trivia

Richard Lederer's
Literary
Trivia

By Richard Lederer

Illustrations by Barry Blitt

Gibbs Smith, Publisher

TO ENRICH AND INSPIRE HUMANKIND

Salt Lake City | Charleston | Santa Fe | Santa Barbara

First Edition
11 10 09 08 07   5 4 3 2 1

Text © 2007 Richard Lederer
Illustrations © 2007 Barry Blitt

Published by
Gibbs Smith, Publisher
P.O. Box 667
Layton, Utah 84041

Orders: 1.800.835.4993
www.gibbs-smith.com

Designed by Kurt Wahlner
Printed and bound in United States of America

Library of Congress Cataloging-in-Publication Data

Lederer, Richard, 1938-.
Richard Lederer's literary trivia / Richard Lederer ; illustrations by
Barry Blitt. — 1st ed.
    p. cm.
  ISBN-13: 978-1-4236-0211-8
  ISBN-10: 1-4236-0211-0
  1. Literature—Miscellanea. I. Title.

PN43.L385 2007
800–dc22

                              2007003010

To my Haverford College English professors,
who helped me to discover who I am
and why I was put on this planet

Contents

Introduction

Literature lives. Literature endures. Literature prevails. That's because readers bestow a special kind of life upon people who have existed only in books. Figments though they may be, literary characters can assume a vitality and longevity that pulse more powerfully than flesh and blood.

After many years, the publishers of the children's classic *Charlotte's Web* persuaded E. B. White to record his book on tape. So caught had the author become in the web of his arachnid heroine's life that it took nineteen tapings before White could read aloud the passage about Charlotte's death without his voice cracking.

A century earlier, another writer had been deeply affected by the fate of his heroine. Like most of Charles Dickens's works, *The Old Curiosity Shop* (1841) was published in serial form. The novel won a vast readership on both sides of the Atlantic, and as interest in the fate of the heroine, Little Nell, grew intense, circulation reached the staggering figure of 100,000, a record unequaled by any other of Dickens's major novels. In New York, 6,000 people crowded the wharf where the ship carrying the final *Master Humphrey's Clock* magazine installment was due to dock. As it approached, the crowd's impatience grew to such a pitch that they cried out as one to the sailors, "Does Little Nell die?"

Alas, Little Nell did die, and tens of thousands of readers' hearts broke. The often ferocious literary critic Lord Jeffrey was found weeping with his head on his library table. "You'll be sorry to hear," he sobbed to a friend, "that little Nelly, Boz's little Nelly, is dead." Daniel O'Connell, an Irish M.P., burst out crying, "He should not have killed her," and then, in anguish, threw the book out of the window of the train in which he was traveling. A diary of the time records another reader lamenting, "The villain! The rascal! The bloodthirsty scoundrel! He killed my little Nell! He killed my sweet little child!"

That "bloodthirsty scoundrel" was himself shattered by the loss of his heroine. In a letter to a friend Dickens wrote, "I am the wretchedest of the wretched. It [Nell's death] casts the most horrible shadow upon me, and it is as much as I can do to keep moving at all. Nobody will miss her like I shall."

Even more famous than Charlotte and Little Nell is Sir Arthur Conan Doyle's Sherlock Holmes, the world's first consulting detective. The intrepid sleuth's deerstalker hat, Inverness cape, calabash pipe, and magnifying glass are recognized by readers everywhere, and the stories have been translated into more than sixty languages, from Arabic to Yiddish.

In December of 1887, Sherlock Holmes came into the world as an unheralded and unnoticed Yuletide child in *Beeton's Christmas Annual*. When, not long after, *The Strand Magazine* began the monthly serialization of the first dozen short stories entitled "The Adventures of Sherlock Holmes," the issues sold tens of thousands and the public furiously clamored for more.

At the height of success, however, the creator wearied of his creation. He yearned for "higher writing" and felt his special calling to be the historical novel. In December 1893, Doyle introduced the arch criminal Professor James Moriarty into the last story in the Memoirs series. In "The Final Problem," Holmes and the evil professor wrestle at a cliff's edge in Switzerland. Grasping each other frantically, sleuth and villain plummet to their watery deaths at the foot of the Reichenbach Falls.

With Holmes forever destroyed, Doyle felt he could abandon his mystery stories and turn his authorial eyes to the romantic landscapes of the Middle Ages. He longed to chronicle the clangor of medieval battles, the derring-do of brave knights, and the sighs of lovesick maidens. But the writer's tour back in time would not be that easily booked: Sherlock Holmes had taken on a life of his own, something larger than the will of his creator. The normally staid, stiff-upper-lipped British public was first bereaved, then outraged. Conservative London stockbrokers went to work wearing black armbands in mourning for the loss of their heroic detective. Citizens poured out torrents of letters to editors complaining of Holmes's fate. One woman picketed Doyle's home with a sign branding him a murderer.

The appeals of *The Strand*'s publishers to Doyle's sensibilities and purse went unheeded. For the next eight years Holmes lay dead at the bottom of the Swiss falls while Doyle branched out into historical fiction, science-fiction, horror stories, and medical stories. But he wasn't very good at "higher writing."

Finally, Doyle could resist the pressures from publisher and public no more. "The Return of Sherlock Holmes," the series of thirteen stories that brought back Doyle's hero, was greeted eagerly by patient British readers, and the author continued writing stories of his detective right into 1927. When, in 1930, Sir Arthur Conan Doyle died at age 71, readers around the world mourned his passing. Newspaper cartoons portraying a grieving Sherlock Holmes captured the public's sense of irreparable loss.

Such is the power of mythic literature that the creation has outlived his creator. Letters and packages from all over the world still come addressed to "Sherlock Holmes" at 221-B Baker Street, where they are answered by a full-time secretary. Only Santa Claus gets more mail, at least just before Christmastime. More movies, well over three hundred of them, have been made about Holmes than about Dracula, Frankenstein, Robin Hood, and Rocky combined. Sherlock Holmes stories written by post-Doylean authors now vastly outnumber the sixty that Doyle produced. More than one hundred and fifty societies in homage to Sherlock Holmes are active in the United States alone.

However many times the progenitor tried to finish off his hero, by murder or retirement or flat refusal to write any more adventures, the Great Detective lives, vigilant and deductive as ever, protecting the humble from the evils that lurk in the very heart of our so-called civilization. Despite his "death" more than a hundred years ago, Sherlock Holmes has never died. Readers around the world simply won't let him.

If you have read this far in this introduction, you are almost certainly a person for whom the people who live in books are very much alive. *Literary Trivia* will show just how much fun the study of great—and sometimes more-popular-than-great—literature can be. When you are done reading this book and playing the games, you may be inspired to read or reread some of the masterpieces mentioned along the way. If you are, run—don't walk—to your nearest library.

Richard Lederer
San Diego, California
richard.lederer@pobox.com

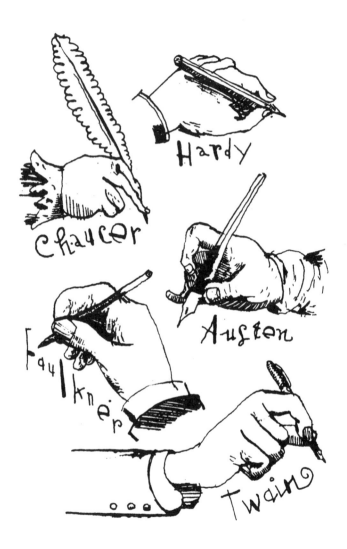

Chaucer

Hardy

Austen

Faulkner

Twain

Authors

Authorial Anecdotes

Henry David Thoreau, who wrote *Walden*, helped runaway slaves escape to Canada and became one of the first Americans to speak in defense of John Brown. When Thoreau spent a day in jail for acting on the dictates of his conscience, he was visited by friend Ralph Waldo Emerson.

Emerson asked, "Henry, why are you here?"

Thoreau answered, "Waldo, why are you *not* here?"

Within the brief compass of a biographical incident we can sometimes catch and crystallize the essence of a person's character. Here are some famous episodes from the lives of famous authors, each of whom you are asked to identify:

1. When he was 90 years of age, this Greek tragedian was brought before a court of law by his sons, who sought to have him declared senile and thus incompetent to manage his estate. In his own defense, the playwright read aloud passages from his *Oedipus at Colonus,* which he had recently completed but not yet staged. The jury confirmed his competency, chastised his sons, and escorted him home as an honor.

2. President Abraham Lincoln took this abolitionist author of *Uncle Tom's Cabin* by the hand and asked, "So this is the little lady who made this big war."

3. This British writer's rags-to-riches life was more remarkable than any of his sentimental stories. Born into an impoverished family and having worked as a child slave in a London blacking factory, he became, at the age of twenty-five, the most popular author in England.

4. Unemployed and living on state benefits, this single mother wrote much of her first novel sitting in local Edinburgh cafes and banging

away on a manual typewriter in her sister's home. By the time she had completed six of the seven books in her projected series, she was named "the greatest living British writer"—and she certainly has become by far the richest.

5. This reclusive American writer was depicted in W. P. Kinsella's novel *Shoeless Joe.* When the subject threatened to sue, he was replaced in the film version, titled *Field of Dreams,* by a fictitious writer named Terrence Mann, who was portrayed by James Earl Jones.

6. This writer, critic, and humorist once arrived simultaneously at a narrow doorway with the playwright, journalist, and politician Clare Boothe Luce.

"Age before beauty," said Mrs. Luce, stepping aside.

"Pearls before swine," purred our writer as she glided through the doorway.

7. Born a slave in Maryland and escaping in 1838, this powerful orator became the leading African American in the abolitionist movement. He recruited black soldiers to fight in the Civil War and ultimately produced three autobiographies.

8. At the height of this British writer's popularity, he is said to have earned about a dollar a word. This inspired a certain autograph hound, who had been unsuccessful in obtaining the great man's signature, to try again. He sent off a letter that he was sure would produce the desired result: "I see you get $1 a word for your writing. I enclose a check for $1. Please send me a sample." The writer replied by postcard—unsigned—"Thanks."

9. In less than nine years, this London man of letters almost single-handedly produced the first authoritative dictionary of the English language, a feat that took academy committees in France and Italy decades to accomplish.

10. This politically active English poet became completely blind at the age of forty-five and afterward wrote a sonnet, "On His Blindness," and the epic poem *Paradise Lost*.

11. This English Lake Poet fell asleep, perhaps under the influence of opium, and dreamt a complete vision of a poem, "Kubla Khan." When he awoke, he immediately set to writing out his vision but was interrupted by "a person on business from Porlock."

12. The poet Lord Byron challenged a group of his friends to create their own ghost stories. From that challenge came the tale *Frankenstein,* written by this twenty-one-year-old wife of another romantic poet.

13. When the first edition of this American poet's collection of poems appeared in 1855, the *Boston Intelligencer* said in its review: "The author should be kicked out from all decent society as below the level of the brute. He must be some escaped lunatic raving in pitiable delirium." The collection went through nine more editions and gained a large, enthusiastic readership in the United States and England.

14. Only seven of this New England woman's poems were published during her lifetime, and she left instructions that all of her manuscripts be destroyed after her death. Today she and her contemporary in the question above are the two most widely read and influential American poets of the nineteenth century.

15. This New England writer had 706 copies of one of his unsold books returned to him by a book dealer. In a journal entry he wrote, "I now

have a library of nearly 900 volumes, over 700 of which I wrote myself."

16. This American humorist and member of the famed Algonquin Round Table once quipped, "It took me fifteen years to discover that I had no talent for writing, but I couldn't give it up because by that time I was too famous."

17. Worn down by poverty, this once-unknown Scottish poet resolved to immigrate to Jamaica in 1786. To finance the journey, he gathered together some of his poems in a thin volume. The small collection took Scotland by storm, and the young man went on to become his country's national poet.

18. This London pre-Romantic poet was also a painter, engraver, and spiritual visionary. He was struck with what is known as eidetic sight, a quality that allowed him to see visions as well as imagine them. When he was but a child, he claimed to have seen the prophet Ezekiel in a tree. His vivid engravings designed to accompany his poems made him the world's first multimedia artist.

19. As a young cadet, this American writer was expelled from West Point for reporting to a march wearing nothing but white gloves.

20. This British writer showed his first novel, *The White Peacock,* to his coal-miner father. After struggling through half a page, the father asked, "And what dun they gie thee for that, lad?"

"Fifty pounds, Father," the son answered.

"Fifty pounds!" exclaimed the dumbfounded father. "Fifty pounds! An' tha's niver done a day's hard work in thy life!"

21. When he was a young busboy in a Washington, D. C., hotel, this American poet left a packet of his poems next to the poet Vachel Lindsay's plate. Lindsay helped to launch the young man's career, and the busboy became the leading figure in the Harlem Renaissance.

22. and 23. When a popular Jazz Age American novelist remarked to another famous writer that "the rich are very different from you and me," the latter replied, "Yes, they have more money." Name the two authors.

24. When this Russian writer's first novel was well received in 1846, he joined a revolu-

tionary group that was infiltrated by the authorities. Together with several associates, he was tried and sentenced to be shot. The execution was a cruel hoax, and, at the very last minute, the sentence was commuted to years of hard labor in Siberia. Ten years later he returned to St. Petersburg as a conservative and became one of the very greatest of all Russian authors.

25. When this Irish playwright was stopped by U.S. customs in New York, he proclaimed, "I have nothing to declare except my genius."

26. A 19-month-old girl lay dying in a London hospital. Her condition baffled the doctors until a nurse noted that the patient's symptoms were remarkably like those of an infant in the detective novel *The Pale Horse*. The nurse's suggestion that the patient could have thallium poisoning was confirmed by tests. Given proper treatment, the baby recovered. Who was the famous author of *The Pale Horse*?

27. This conjurer of animal fables is said to have been a deformed black slave who lived in the sixth century B.C. According to tradition, he

used his fables to bolster his arguments and, ultimately, to win his freedom.

28. The science-fiction stories of this French author were called "dreams come true." So prophetic was his description of a periscope in *Twenty Thousand Leagues Under the Sea* that a few years later the actual inventor of the instrument was refused permission for an original patent.

29. After reaching age 40, this housewife and mother of five began writing her first books—the Earth's Children fictional saga. The series has gone on to become one of the best-selling in publishing history.

30. This American poet was asked to compose a poem and read it at John F. Kennedy's inauguration in 1961. When the sun's glare prevented him from reading the poem at the occasion, he instead recited "The Gift Outright" from memory.

Answers

1. Sophocles 2. Harriet Beecher Stowe
3. Charles Dickens 4. J. K. Rowling
5. J. D. Salinger 6. Dorothy Parker
7. Frederick Douglass 8. Rudyard Kipling
9. Samuel Johnson 10. John Milton

11. Samuel Taylor Coleridge
12. Mary Wollstonecraft Shelley
13. Walt Whitman 14. Emily Dickinson
15. Henry David Thoreau
16. Robert Benchley 17. Robert Burns
18. William Blake 19. Edgar Allan Poe
20. D. H. Lawrence

21. Langston Hughes
22. and 23. F. Scott Fitzgerald
    and Ernest Hemingway
24. Fyodor Dostoevsky 25. Oscar Wilde
26. Agatha Christie 27. Aesop
28. Jules Verne 29. Jean Auel
30. Robert Frost

Author!
Author!
Author!

On a February day in 1892, Charles Buzzell, who had lain unconscious for nine days without food and water, was virtually DOA by the time he got to St. Vincent's Hospital. Doctors in the emergency room battled the odds to keep him alive—and won. The heroism of the medical staff so impressed Buzzell's married sister that when she gave birth to a daughter not long thereafter, she honored the institution by making it part of the baby's name. That's how poet

Edna St. Vincent Millay came to be named—in dactylic trimeter!—for a New York hospital.

Edna St. Vincent Millay is a trinomial, that is, a person who is best known by three names. To gain a glimpse into an age when trinomials were more in fashion, look at the middle names of dead poets and other writers who were best known by three names:

1. _____ Allan _____

2. _____ Anne _____

3. _____ Arlington _____

4. _____ Barrett _____

5. _____ Bashevis _____

6. _____ Beecher _____

7. _____ Bernard _____

8. _____ Butler _____

9. _____ Bysshe _____

10. _____ Carlos _____

11. _____ Chandler _____

12. _____ Christian _____

13. _____ Clarke _____

14. _____   Conan   _____

15. _____   David   _____

16. _____   Fenimore   _____

17. _____   Ingalls   _____

18. _____   Kinnan   _____

19. _____   Laurence   _____

20. _____   Lee   _____

21. _____   Louis   _____

22. _____   Makepeace   _____

23. _____   May   _____

24. _____   Neale   _____

25. _____   Penn   _____

26. _____   Rice   _____

27. _____   Stanley   _____

28. _____   Taylor   _____

29. _____   Wadsworth   _____

30. _____   Waldo   _____

31. _____   Ward   _____

32. _____   Weldon   _____

33. _____   Wendell   _____

34. _____ Wollstonecraft _____

Answers

1. Edgar Poe 2. Katherine Porter
3. Edwin Robinson 4. Elizabeth Browning
5. Isaac Singer 6. Harriet Stowe
7. George Shaw 8. William Yeats
9. Percy Shelley 10. William Williams

11. Joel Harris 12. Hans Andersen
13. Clement Moore 14. Arthur Doyle
15. Henry Thoreau 16. James Cooper
17. Laura Wilder 18. Marjorie Rawlings
19. Paul Dunbar 20. Edgar Masters

21. Robert Stevenson 22. William Thackeray
23. Louisa Alcott 24. Zora Hurston
25. Robert Warren 26. Edgar Burroughs
27. Erle Gardner 28. Samuel Coleridge
29. Henry Longfellow 30. Ralph Emerson

31. Julia Howe or Henry Beecher
32. James Johnson 33. Oliver Holmes
34. Mary Shelley

Letter-Perfect Writers

Other writers prefer to be known by their initials rather than their full names. Take the initiative and match the writerly initials in the left-hand column with the last names in the right-hand column:

1.	A. A.	Andrews
2.	A. E.	Auden
3.	C. S.	Cummings
4.	D. H.	Doctorow.
5.	E. B.	Du Bois
6.	E. E.	Eliot

7.	E. L.	Forster
8.	E. M.	Frank Baum
9.	F.	Henry
10.	H. G.	Hinton
11.	H. L.	Housman
12.	H. P.	James
13.	J. D.	Lawrence
14.	J. K.	Lewis
15.	J. R. R.	Lovecraft
16.	L.	Mencken
17.	O.	Milne
18.	P. D.	Perelman
19.	P. G.	Rowling
20.	R. L.	Salinger
21.	S. E.	Scott Fitzgerald
22.	S. J.	Somerset Maugham
23.	T. S.	Stein
24.	V. C.	Tolkien
25.	W.	Wells
26.	W. E. B.	White
27.	W. H.	Wodehouse

Answers

1. Milne 2. Housman
3. Lewis 4. Lawrence
5. White 6. Cummings
7. Doctorow 8. Forster
9. Scott Fitzgerald 10. Wells

11. Mencken 12. Lovecraft
13. Salinger 14. Rowling
15. Tolkien 16. Frank Baum
17. Henry 18. James
19. Wodehouse 20. Stein

21. Hinton 22. Perelman
23. Eliot 24. Andrews
25. Somerset Maugham
26. Du Bois 27. Auden

Pen-Ultimate Names

The authors of *Alice's Adventures in Wonderland, Silas Marner,* and *Nineteen Eighty-Four* have something in common besides being British. They are all better known by their pseudonyms, or pen names, than by their real names.

It's hard to imagine why a writer who goes to the trouble of scratching out a work of art would want to be known by another identity. On the other hand, if you were born Amandine Lucie Aurore Dupin, Jacques Anatole Francois Thibault, or Aleksey Maximovich Peshkov, you might adopt the nom de plume of George Sand,

Anatole France, or Maxim Gorky. And, if it's efficiency you seek, it's obvious that Moliere, Voltaire, and Stendhal are considerably more compact than Jean-Baptiste Poquelin, Francois-Marie Arouet, and Marie Henri Beyle.

Here are brief biographies of fifteen famous writers who made the change. From the information supplied, identify each pseudonym:

1. Eric Arthur Blair wrote a long fable about a society in which some animals are more equal than others. In 1948, he published a novel about a nightmarish society of the future, one in which everybody had a Big Brother.

2. Samuel Langhorne Clemens was a steamboat pilot before he became a writer. In 1863, he took on the pen name that was a nostalgic reminder of his riverboat days.

3. In March 1836, what has been described as the most successful writing career in history was launched with the publication of *The Posthumous Papers of the Pickwick Club*. The author, of course, was Charles Dickens. In 1833, when he was only twenty-one, Dickens began contributing stories

and essays to magazines and published them pseudonymously in a collection called *Sketches by* _____.

4. Charles Lutwidge Dodgson was fascinated with words, logic, and little girls. Out of these interests he fashioned a wonderland of characters—Humpty Dumptys, Jabberwocks, Mad Hatters, and White Rabbits.

5. Famous for her novels describing life in nineteenth-century England, including *Adam Bede, Silas Marner,* and *Middlemarch,* Mary Ann Evans adopted a masculine pen name, by George.

6. He meant what he said, and he said what he meant, and his books have pleased children one hundred percent. Theodor Giesel conjured up and drew creatures that now exist in the imaginations of generations of children.

7. Convicted of embezzlement, William Sydney Porter spent almost four years in prison, where he began his career as an immensely popular writer of short stories. Most of his tales are about life in New York and are marked by surprise endings.

8. Late in life, after a long career as a veterinary surgeon, James Alfred Wight began writing books that communicated his profound affection for animals. The titles of two of those books are taken from a hymn that begins, "All things bright and beautiful, all creatures great and small."

9. Jozef Korzeniowski was born in Poland and grew up speaking no English until he was seventeen, yet he became one of the greatest stylists ever to use the English language. A sailor as a youth, Korzeniowski is most famous for his stories and novels of the sea.

10. Hector Hugh Munro was killed in action during World War I. He left behind him the charming, often biting short stories to which he signed a pseudonym borrowed from *The Rubáiyát*.

11. An unpublished Atlanta writer named Peggy Marsh submitted an incomplete manuscript that filled a large suitcase. The title of the novel was to be *Tomorrow Is Another Day*, and its heroine was to be called Pansy. After a great number of changes, including the title and

name of the heroine, the book was published in 1936 and quickly became an all-time best seller, inspiring a blockbuster movie, and, fifty years after that, a blockbuster sequel.

12. Russian-born Yiddish author Solomon Rabinowitz took his pen name from a Hebrew expression meaning "peace be unto you."

13. British novelist and critic John B. Wilson is most famous for *A Clockwork Orange*. His works often combine word play and a grim view of life.

14. Baroness Karen Blixen, a Danish author who wrote primarily in English, managed a coffee plantation in British East Africa. She is best known for her tales and autobiography drawn from her African experiences.

15. For many years, Manfred Lee and his cousin Frederic Dannay functioned as one author, an eccentric bookworm who allegedly wrote about his adventures as a detective.

Answers

1. George Orwell
2. Mark Twain
3. Boz
4. Lewis Carroll
5. George Eliot

6. Dr. Seuss
7. O. Henry
8. James Herriot
9. Joseph Conrad
10. Saki

11. Margaret Mitchell
12. Sholem Aleichem
13. Anthony Burgess
14. Isak Dinesen
15. Ellery Queen

Titles

The Mother
of All Titles

How many works have you read whose titles contain the preposition *of*, particularly the pattern *noun of a noun?* So many literary titles are cut from this fabricated cloth that the fifty in the game you are about to play are just a tiny sample.

The *noun of a noun* pattern is so formulaic that we can present each title and author as a formula. Thus, "The F of the H of U, by Edgar Allan Poe" and "The M of V, by William Shakespeare" reveal themselves as "The Fall of the House of Usher" and *The Merchant of Venice*.

In taking this kind of test, most people solve

fewer than half the problems on their first try, but they find that insights into additional answers come to them in sudden flashes when they return to the task a second or third time. The clues provided may be initially (get the pun?) confusing, but persevere and you will identify many, perhaps most, of the encrypted titles:

1. The A of H F,
    by Mark Twain

2. The A of M X,
    by Alex Haley

3. The B of M C,
    by Robert James Waller

4. The B of the V,
    by Tom Wolfe

5. The C of A,
    by Edgar Allan Poe

6. The C of L 49,
    by Thomas Pynchon

7. The C of M C,
    by Alexandre Dumas

8. The C of the C B,
    by Jean Auel

9. The C of N T,
    by William Styron

10. The C of the W,
    by Jack London

11. D of a S,
    by Arthur Miller

12. The D of a Y G,
    by Anne Frank

13. F of F,
    by Erica Jong

14. The G of W,
    by John Steinbeck

15. The H of B A,
    by Federico Garcia Lorca

16. H of D,
    by Joseph Conrad

17. The H of M,
    by Edith Wharton

18. The H of N D,
    by Victor Hugo

19. The H of the B,
    by Sir Arthur Conan Doyle

20. The H of the S G,
      by Nathaniel Hawthorne

21. The I of B E,
      by Oscar Wilde

22. The I of the K,
      by Alfred, Lord Tennyson

23. L of G,
      by Walt Whitman

24. The L of S H,
      by Washington Irving

25. L of the F,
      by William Golding

26. The L of the M,
      by James Fenimore Cooper

27. L of the R,
      by J. R. R. Tolkien

28. The M of C,
      by Thomas Hardy

29. The N of the R,
      by Umberto Eco

30. P of the A,
      by Pierre Boulle

31. The P of M J B,
    by Muriel Spark

32. The P of T,
    by Pat Conroy

33. A P of the A as a Y M,
    by James Joyce

34. The R B of C,
    by Stephen Crane

35. The R of S L,
    by William Dean Howells

36. R of T P,
    by Marcel Proust

37. The R of the A M,
    by Samuel Taylor Coleridge

38. The R of the L,
    by Alexander Pope

39. The S L of W M,
    by James Thurber

40. The S of B F,
    by W. E. B. Dubois

41. S of F,
    by Katherine Anne Porter

42. The S of K,
    by Ernest Hemingway

43. The S of O T,
      by Thornton Wilder

44. S of S,
      by Toni Morrison

45. The S of the L,
      by Thomas Harris

46. T of the A,
      by Edgar Rice Burroughs

47. A T of T C,
      by Charles Dickens

48. The W of the H,
      by Henry Wadsworth Longfellow

49. The W of the W,
      by H. G. Wells

50. The W W of O,
      by L. Frank Baum

Bonus question:

The T of the S, by
Henry James,
William Shakespeare,
and E. B. White.

Identify all three titles.

Answers

1. *The Adventures of Huckleberry Finn* 2. *The Autobiography of Malcolm X* 3. *The Bridges of Madison County* 4. *The Bonfire of the Vanities* 5. "The Cask of Amontillado"

6. *The Crying of Lot 49* 7. *The Count of Monte Cristo* 8. *The Clan of the Cave Bear* 9. *The Confessions of Nat Turner* 10. *The Call of the Wild*

11. *Death of a Salesman* 12. *The Diary of a Young Girl* 13. *Fear of Flying* 14. *The Grapes of Wrath* 15. *The House of Bernardo Alba*

16. *Heart of Darkness* 17. *The House of Mirth* 18. *The Hunchback of Notre Dame* 19. "The Hound of the Baskervilles" 20. *The House of the Seven Gables*

21. *The Importance of Being Earnest* 22. "The Idylls of the King" 23. *Leaves of Grass* 24. "The Legend of Sleepy Hollow" 25. *Lord of the Flies*

26. *The Last of the Mohicans* 27. *Lord of the Rings* 28. *The Mayor of Casterbridge* 29. *The Name of the Rose* 30. *Planet of the Apes*

31. *The Prime of Miss Jean Brodie* 32. *The Prince of Tides* 33. *A Portrait of the Artist as a Young Man* 34. *The Red Badge of Courage* 35. *The Rise of Silas Lapham*

36. *Remembrance of Things Past* 37. *The Rime of the Ancient Mariner* 38. "The Rape of the Lock" 39. "The Secret Life of Walter Mitty" 40. *The Souls of Black Folk*

41. *Ship of Fools* 42. "The Snows of Kilimanjaro" 43. *The Skin of Our Teeth* 44. *Song of Solomon* 45. *The Silence of the Lambs*

46. *Tarzan of the Apes* 47. *A Tale of Two Cities* 48. "The Wreck of the Hesperus" 49. *The War of the Worlds* 50. *The Wonderful Wizard of Oz*

Bonus question: *The Turn of the Screw, The Taming of the Shrew,* and *The Trumpet of the Swan*

Heavyweight Titles

When writers create titles for their works, they draw their ideas from many sources — including the works of writers who have come before them. Take Ernest Hemingway as an example. He wrote a big novel about a man's personal commitment to a struggling people during the Spanish Civil War, and he sought a title that would express the interdependence of all men and women. Hemingway eventually found that title in a meditation composed by the early seventeenth-century writer John Donne: "Any man's death diminishes me because I am involved in mankind, and therefore never send to know for whom the bell tolls; it tolls for thee."

Hemingway titled his novel *For Whom the Bell Tolls*.

Here are thirty literary passages, each of which inspired the title of another famous literary work that came after. Identify the title inspired by each passage and the author of each work:

1. Mine eyes have seen the glory
   Of the coming of the Lord;
   He is tramping out the vintage
   Where the grapes of wrath are stored.
   — Julia Ward Howe,
   "Battle Hymn of the Republic"

2. What happens to a dream deferred?
   Does it dry up
   Like a raisin in the sun?
   — Langston Hughes, "Harlem"

3 John Brown's body lies a-moldering
      in the grave,
   His soul is marching on.
   — Thomas Brigham Bishop,
   "John Brown's Body"

4. Humpty Dumpty sat on a wall:
    Humpty Dumpty had a great fall.
    All the King's horses and all the King's men
    Couldn't put Humpty Dumpty
        back together again.

    — nursery rhyme

5. Look homeward, Angel, now, and melt
        with ruth:
    And o ye dolphins, waft the hapless
        youth.

    — John Milton, "Lycidas"

6. Far from the madding crowd's
        ignoble strife,
    Their sober wishes never learned to stray;
    Along the cool sequestered vale of life
    They kept the noiseless tenor of their way.

    — Thomas Gray,
    "Elegy Written in a Country Churchyard"

7. It Beareth the name of Vanity-Fair,
    because the town where 'tis kept, is
    lighter than Vanity.

    — John Bunyan, *The Pilgrim's Progress*

8. Away! away! for I will fly to thee,
   Not charioted by Bacchus and his pards,
   But on the viewless wings of poesy,
   Though the dull brain perplexes and
       retards
   Already with thee! tender is the night.
   — John Keats, "Ode to a Nightingale"

9. The best laid schemes o' mice an' men,
   Gang aft a-gley,
   An' lea'e us naught but grief an' pain
   For promised joy!
   — Robert Burns, "To a Mouse"

10. It is not a carol of joy or glee,
    But a prayer that he sends from his heart's
        deep core,
    But a plea, that upward to heaven he
        flings —
    I know why the caged bird sings!
    — Paul Laurence Dunbar, "Sympathy"

11. Go down Moses, way down to Egypt land.
    Tell old Pharaoh: Let my people go.
    —African American spiritual

12. Of arms and the man I sing
    — Vergil, *Aeneid*

13. One flew east, one flew west,
   One flew over the cuckoo's nest.
   — nursery rhyme

14. "You and me, we've made a separate
   peace."
   — Ernest Hemingway, "A Very Short Story"

15. I have forgot much, Cynara! gone with the
      wind,
   Flung roses, roses riotously with the
      throng,
   Dancing, to put thy pale, lost lilies out of
      mind.
                    — Ernest Dowson, "Cynara"

16. Turning and turning in the widening gyre
   The falcon cannot hear the falconer;
   Things fall apart; the centre cannot hold;
   Mere anarchy is loosed upon the world.
                    — William Butler Yeats,
                       "The Second Coming"

17. Gentlemen-rankers out on the spree,
    Damned from here to Eternity,
    God ha' mercy on such as we,
    Ba! Yah! Bah!
       — Rudyard Kipling, "Gentlemen-Rankers"

18. Seize the day, put no trust in the morrow!
       — Horace, *Odes,* Book I, Ode xi

19. And what rough beast, its hour come
       round at last,
    Slouches towards Bethlehem to be born?
                — William Butler Yeats,
                   "The Second Coming"

20. I will find out where she has gone
    And kiss her lips and take her hands;
    And walk among long dappled grass,
    And pluck till time and times are done
    The silver apples of the moon,
    The golden apples of the sun.
                — William Butler Yeats,
             "The Song of Wandering Aengus"

21. Well this side of Paradise! . . .
    There's little comfort in the wise.
                — Rupert Brooke, "Tiare Tahiti"

22. Oh, bang the drum slowly and play the
    fife lowly,

    And play the Dead March as you carry me
    along;

    Take me to the green valley, there lay the
    sod o'er me,

    For I'm a young cowboy, and I know I've
    done wrong.

    — Anon., "The Cowboy's Lament"

23. Though nothing can bring back the hour
    Of splendor in the grass, of glory in the
    flower.

    — William Wordsworth,
    "Intimations of Immortality"

24. Between the dark and the daylight,
    When the night is beginning to lower,
    Comes a pause in the day's occupations
    That is known as the Children's Hour.

    — Henry Wadsworth Longfellow,
    "The Children's Hour"

25. I [Death] was astonished to see him in
    Baghdad, for I had an appointment with
    him tomorrow in Samarra.

    — W. Somerset Maugham, *Sheppy*

26. When a true genius appears in the world,
    you may know him by this sign, that the
    dunces are all in confederacy against him.
    — Jonathan Swift, "Thoughts on Various
                    Subjects, Moral and Diverting"

27. Cast a cold eye
    On life, on death.
    Horseman, pass by!
    — William Butler Yeats, "Under Ben Bulben"

28. A Book of Verses underneath the Bough,
    A Jug of Wine, a Loaf of Bread —
        and thou
    Beside me singing in the Wilderness —
    Oh, Wilderness were Paradise enou!
    — Edward FitzGerald, *Rubáiyát of Omar Khayyám*

29. Go tell it on the mountain,
    Over the hills and everywhere,
    Go tell it on the mountain
    That Jesus Christ is born.
                    — African American spiritual

30. Two roads diverged in a wood, and I —
    I took the one less traveled by,
    And that has made all the difference.
                — Robert Frost, "The Road Not Taken"

Answers

1. John Steinbeck, *The Grapes of Wrath*
2. Lorraine Hansberry, *A Raisin in the Sun*
3. Stephen Vincent Benet, *John Brown's Body*
4. Robert Penn Warren, *All the King's Men*
5. Thomas Wolfe, *Look Homeward, Angel*
6. Thomas Hardy, *Far from the Madding Crowd*
7. William Makepeace Thackeray, *Vanity Fair*
8. F. Scott Fitzgerald, *Tender Is the Night* 9. John Steinbeck, *Of Mice and Men* 10. Maya Angelou, *I Know Why the Caged Bird Sings*

11. William Faulkner, *Go Down, Moses*
12. George Bernard Shaw, *Arms and the Man*
13. Ken Kesey, *One Flew Over the Cuckoo's Nest*
14. John Knowles, *A Separate Peace* 15. Margaret Mitchell, *Gone with the Wind* 16. Chinua

Achebe, *Things Fall Apart* 17. James Jones, *From Here to Eternity* 18. Saul Bellow, *Seize the Day* 19. Joan Didion, *Slouching Towards Bethlehem* 20. Ray Bradbury, *The Golden Apples of the Sun* (also Eudora Welty, *The Golden Apples*, Marjorie Kinnan Rawlings, *Golden Apples*)

21. F. Scott Fitzgerald, *This Side of Paradise* 22. Mark Harris, *Bang the Drum Slowly* . . . 23. William Inge, *Splendor in the Grass* 24. Lillian Hellman, *The Children's Hour* 25. John O'Hara, *An Appointment in Samarra* 26. John Kennedy Toole, *A Confederacy of Dunces* 27. Larry McMurtry, *Horseman, Pass By!* and Mary McCarthy, *Cast a Cold Eye* 28. Eugene O'Neill, *Ah, Wilderness!* 29. James Baldwin, *Go Tell It on the Mountain* 30. M. Scott Peck, *The Road Less Traveled*

Title
Search

Master storyteller W. Somerset Maugham once revealed how he constructed his many titles: "A good title is apt, specific, attractive, new, and short." In addition to these recommended qualities, some famous titles possess intrigue by inviting us into the books they name so that we can find out what the title actually means.

For many readers, the title *One Flew Over the Cuckoo's Nest* seems to be no more than a casual reference to a children's folk rhyme. Others are drawn by the contradiction embedded in Ken Kesey's title into the eccentric, polarized world of the novel. Cuckoos do not build nests; they lay their eggs in the nests of other birds. The contradiction mirrors the central irrationality of the novel itself, in which the bars separating the sane and insane, saints and sinners, and watchers and watched waver and blur.

Answer each of the following questions to show how the meanings of literary titles are often revealed in the works they announce:

1. What is the prize in Shirley Jackson's story "The Lottery"?

2. Who is Charley in John Steinbeck's *Travels with Charley*?

3. Who is *The Catcher in the Rye* in J. D. Salinger's novel and why is he a catcher?

4. Why did George Orwell choose *Nineteen Eighty-Four* as the title and year of his novel?

5. Who is Algernon in Daniel Keyes's *Flowers for Algernon*?

6. In Joseph Heller's novel, what is *Catch-22*?

7. In T. S. Eliot's play *Murder in the Cathedral*, who was murdered?

8. What is *Mrs. Warren's Profession* in George Bernard Shaw's play by that name?

9. In what army is Shaw's *Major Barbara* a soldier?

10. What are the two cities in Charles Dickens's *A Tale of Two Cities*?

11. Why did Samuel Butler name his utopia *Erewhon*?

12. What is "The Windhover" in Gerard Manley Hopkins's poem?

13. In Nathaniel Hawthorne's *The Scarlet Letter*, what is the letter and what does it stand for?

14. What does *R.U.R.* stand for in Karel Capek's play?

15. What does *wuthering* mean in Emily Brontë's *Wuthering Heights*?

16. In Alexsandr Solzhenitsyn's *The Gulag Archipelago*, what do *gulag* and *archipelago* mean?

17. What is *Tono-Bungay* in the title of H. G. Wells's novel?

18. What is the speaker's modest proposal in "A Modest Proposal" by Jonathan Swift?

19. In Robert Browning's "The Pied Piper of Hamelin" and Gerard Manley Hopkins's "Pied Beauty," what does *pied* mean?

20. In William Golding's novel, who or what is the *Lord of the Flies*?

21. What is the jungle in Upton Sinclair's *The Jungle?*

22. In Stendhal's *The Charterhouse of Parma,* what is a charterhouse?

23. In Sir Arthur Conan Doyle's "The Five Orange Pips," what are pips?

24. In *Out of the Silent Planet* and *Perelandra,* the next novel in the trilogy, what two planets is C. S. Lewis referring to in his titles?

25. What is the talisman in Sir Walter Scott's *The Talisman?*

26. What is the lock in Alexander Pope's "The Rape of the Lock" and how was it "raped"?

27. What is the folly in Joseph Conrad's *Almayer's Folly?*

28. What is the name of the town in Thornton Wilder's play *Our Town?*

29. What is a scrivener in Herman Melville's story "Bartleby the Scrivener"?

30. What is the octopus in Frank Norris's *The Octopus?*

Mary Chase gave her tall tale a very short title, *Harvey.* Harvey isn't a person; he's a six-foot-one-inch make-believe rabbit seen only by his companion, the eccentric Elwood P. Dowd. The play was almost called *Daisy,* as Chase's original conception was of a four-foot-tall canary with that name.

Other titles do not reveal characters by name. Provide the name of the character referred to in each title:

31. Victor Hugo's *The Hunchback of Notre Dame*
32. James Fenimore Cooper's *The Last of the Mohicans*
33. Robert Bolt's *A Man For All Seasons*
34. Oliver Goldsmith's *The Vicar of Wakefield*
35. D. H. Lawrence's *Lady Chatterley's Lover*
36. Edward Everett Hale's *The Man Without a Country*
37. Alexandre Dumas' *The Three Musketeers*
38. Fyodor Dostoevsky's *The Brothers Karamazov*
39. Louisa May Alcott's *Little Women*
40. Richard Wright's *Native Son*
41. H. G. Wells's *The Invisible Man*
42. Ralph Ellison's *Invisible Man*
43. Oliver Wendell Holmes's *The Autocrat of the Breakfast-Table*
44. John Webster's *The White Devil*
45. Rudyard Kipling's *Stalky and Company*

46. Henry James's *The Portrait of a Lady*

47. Moliere's *The Miser*

48. James Fenimore Cooper's *The Pathfinder*

49. George S. Kaufman and Moss Hart's *The Man Who Came to Dinner*

50. James Joyce's *A Portrait of the Artist as a Young Man*

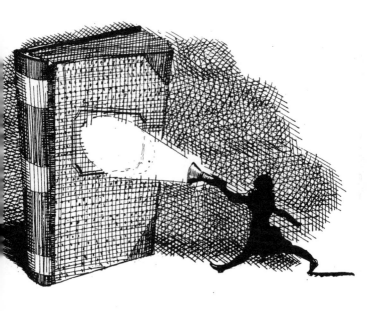

Answers

1. death by stoning 2. Steinbeck's pet poodle 3. Holden Caulfield, who hears the line in the Robert Burns song "If a body meet a body coming through the rye" as "If a body catch a body coming through the rye" 4. Orwell reversed the last two digits of 1948, the year in which he wrote much of the book, in order to show that within a single generation, democracy and freedom could be obliterated. 5. a laboratory rat

6. a military regulation that keeps the pilots in the story flying one suicidal mission after another 7. Thomas à Becket, Archbishop of Canterbury 8. prostitution 9. the Salvation Army 10. London and Paris

11. It's *Nowhere* spelled backward—almost. 12. a kestrel hawk, which hovers so gracefully above the wind 13. *A,* adultery 14. "Rossum's Universal Robots." In 1921 Capek invented the word *robot,* from a Czech root

meaning "to work," for his play. 15. making the sound of wind in the trees

16. *Gulag* is an acronym for the Russian words "Chief Administration of Collective Labor Camps." An archipelago is a cluster of islands, in this case an analogy to the network of prison sites spread throughout Russia. 17. a drug, a phony cure-all 18. that the children of poor people be sold as food for the tables of the rich 19. multicolored, blotched 20. a pig's head on a stick, the devil, or perhaps the darkness of the human heart

21. Chicago's meat-packing district 22. a monastery 23. seeds 24. Earth and Venus 25. an amulet with curative powers

26. a lock of hair of a real-life Miss Arabella Fermor, snipped off by one Robert Lord Petre 27. a house 28. Grover's Corners, New Hampshire 29. a professional copyist or scribe 30. the railroad

31. Quasimodo 32. Chingachgook and his son, Uncas 33. Sir Thomas More 34. Dr. Charles Primrose 35. Oliver Mellors

36. Philip Nolan 37. Athos, Porthos, and Aramis 38. Dimitri, Ivan, Alyosha, and Smerdyakov 39. Meg, Jo, Beth, and Amy March 40. Bigger Thomas

41. Griffin 42. He is never named. 43. Oliver Wendell Holmes 44. Vittoria Corombona 45. Arthur Corkran

46. Isabel Archer 47. Harpagon 48. Natty Bumppo 49. Sheridan Whiteside 50. Stephen Dedalus

Playing the Numbers Game

When a number of books he had lent were not returned, Sir Walter Scott quipped, "My friends may not be good in mathematics, but they are excellent book-keepers." Authors are sometimes unmathematical, but the numbers they place in some of their titles are often significant to the stories themselves.

In Ray Bradbury's *Fahrenheit 451,* for example, the title turns out to be the temperature at which book paper ignites, an important figure in a society that employs firemen not to save houses but to burn down houses—houses suspected of containing books.

Joseph Heller's *Catch-22* refers to a military regulation that keeps pilots flying one suicidal mission after another. ("That's some catch, that Catch-22," observes Yossarian. "It's the best there is," Doc Daneeka agrees.) The only way to be excused from such duty is to be declared insane, but asking to be excepted is proof of a rational mind and bars excuse. The number 22 rhythmically and symbolically captures the double duplicity of both the military code and the bizarre world that Heller shapes in his novel.

Using the name of each author and each embedded number, provide the title of each work:

1. Alexsandr Solzhenitsyn (1)
2. Ken Kesey (1)
3. T. H. White (1)
4. William Shakespeare (2)
5. Charles Dickens (2)
6. Richard Henry Dana (2)
7. Alexandre Dumas (3)
8. Anton Chekhov (3)
9. John Dos Passos (3)
10. T. S. Eliot (4)
11. Sir Arthur Conan Doyle (4)

12. Kurt Vonnegut (5)

13. Ernest Hemingway (5)

14. Sir Arthur Conan Doyle (5)

15. Luigi Pirandello (6)

16. A. A. Milne (6)

17. W. Somerset Maugham (6)

18. Nathaniel Hawthorne (7)

19. Nicholas Meyer (7)

20. Aeschylus (7)

21. T. E. Lawrence (7)

22. Fletcher Knebel and Charles W. Bailey II (7)

23. Richard Wright (8)

24. John O'Hara (8)

25. J. D. Salinger (9)

26. Dorothy L. Sayers (9)

27. Agatha Christie (10)

28. John Reed (10)

29. William Shakespeare (12)

30. Reginald Rose (12)

31. Booth Tarkington (17)

32. Leon Uris (18)

33. A. E. Housman (21)

34. John Buchan (39)

35. John Dos Passos (42)

36. Thomas Pynchon (49)

37. Harold Robbins (79)

38. Jules Verne (80)
39. Helene Hanff (84)
40. Victor Hugo (93)
41. Gabriel Garcia Marquez (100)
42. Dodie Smith (101)
43. Marquis de Sade (120)
44. Arthur Schlesinger (1,000)
45. Arabian folk tales (1,001)
46. Arthur C. Clarke (2,001)
47. Jules Verne (20,000)
48. Ernest Hemingway (50,000)
49. Mark Twain (1,000,000)
50. James Frey (1,000,000)

One of the most enigmatic of number mysteries occurs in a text, not a title. What may well be the most famous of O. Henry's short stories, "The Gift of the Magi" (1906), begins with this sentence: "One dollar and eighty-seven cents. That was all. And sixty cents of it was in pennies."

Do we have here yet another creative but impractical author who has trouble with his math? It is, of course, impossible to make up $1.87 if sixty (rather than sixty-two) cents of it is in pennies.

But not so fast. Turns out that, in the United

States, two- and three-cent pieces were struck during the late nineteenth century and remained in circulation for decades after. Thus, it would have been quite possible in O. Henry's America to have a dollar and eighty-seven cents that did not include any pennies.

Answers

1. *One Day in the Life of Ivan Denisovich* 2. *One Flew Over the Cuckoo's Nest* 3. *The Once and Future King* 4. *Two Gentleman of Verona, The Two Noble Kinsmen* (with John Fletcher) 5. *A Tale of Two Cities* 6. *Two Years Before the Mast* 7. *The Three Musketeers* 8. *The Three Sisters* 9. *Three Soldiers* 10. *Four Quartets*

11. "The Sign of Four" 12. *Slaughterhouse-Five* 13. *The Fifth Column* 14. "The Five Orange Pips" 15. *Six Characters In Search of an Author* 16. *Now We Are Six* 17. *The Moon and Sixpence* 18. *The House of the Seven Gables* 19. *The Seven-Per-Cent Solution* 20. *Seven Against Thebes*

21. *Seven Pillars of Wisdom* 22. *Seven Days in May* 23. *Eight Men* 24. *Butterfield 8* 25. *Nine*

Stories 26. *The Nine Tailors* 27. *Ten Little Indians* 28. *Ten Days That Shook the World* 29. *Twelfth Night* 30. *Twelve Angry Men*

31. *Seventeen* 32. *Mila 18* 33. "When I was One-and-Twenty" 34. *The Thirty-Nine Steps* 35. *The 42nd Parallel* 36. *The Crying of Lot 49* 37. *79 Park Avenue* 38. *Around the World in Eighty Days* 39. *84 Charing Cross Road* 40. *Ninety-Three*

41. *One Hundred Years of Solitude* 42. *101 Dalmatians* 43. *One Hundred Twenty Days of Sodom* 44. *The Thousand Days* 45. *The Thousand and One Nights* 46. *2001: A Space Odyssey* 47. *Twenty Thousand Leagues under the Sea* 48. "Fifty Grand" 49. "The £ 1,000,000 Bank-Note" 50. *A Million Little Pieces*

Works

Try These for Openers

"Write dramatic, button-holing leads to your stories," James Thurber's editor commanded during his early days as a newspaper reporter. In response, Thurber turned in a murder story that began: "Dead. That's what the man was when they found him with a knife in his back at 4 P.M. in front of Riley's Saloon at the corner of 52nd and 12th Streets."

Some beginnings are so effective and well known that readers can look at them and identify the literary works that they lead off. Using the lists of titles and authors that follow, identify the novel or short story started by each sentence and the author of each work:

1. Call me Ishmael.

2. Nothing to be done.

3. It is a truth universally acknowledged, that a single man in possession of a good fortune, must be in want of a wife.

4. It was a bright cold day in April, and the clocks were striking thirteen.

5. Mr. and Mrs. Dursley, of number four, Privet Drive, were proud to say that they were perfectly normal, thank you very much. They were the last people you'd expect to be involved in anything strange or mysterious, because they just didn't hold with such nonsense.

6. Whether I shall turn out to be the hero of my own life, or whether that station will be held by anybody else, these pages must show.

7. It was Wang Lung's marriage day.

8. It was love at first sight.

9. To the red country and part of the gray country of Oklahoma, the last rains came gently, and they did not cut the scarred earth.

10. She was one of those pretty, charming ladies, born, as if through an error of destiny, into a family of clerks.

11. Renowned curator Jacques Saunière staggered through the vaulted archway of the museum's Grand Gallery.

12. As Gregor Samsa awoke one morning from uneasy dreams, he found himself transformed into a giant insect.

13. Buck did not read the newspapers or he would have known that trouble was brewing, not alone for himself, but for every tide-water dog, strong of muscle and with warm, long hair, from Puget Sound to San Diego.

14. The boy with fair hair lowered himself down the last few feet of rock and began to pick his way toward the lagoon.

15. Brrrrrrriiiiiiiiiiiiiiiiiinng!

16. When he was nearly thirteen, my brother Jem got his arm badly broken at the elbow.

17. It was a dark and stormy night . . .

18. They're out there.

19. "Christmas won't be Christmas without any presents," grumbled Jo, lying on the rug.

20. What can you say about a twenty-five-year-old girl who died?

21. He was an old man who fished alone in a skiff in the Gulf Stream and he had gone eighty-four days now without taking a fish.

22. When Mrs. Frederick C. Little's second son arrived, everybody noticed that he was not much bigger than a mouse.

23. A throng of bearded men, in sad-colored garments and gray, steeple-crowned hats, intermixed with women, some wearing hoods, and others bareheaded, was assembled in front of a wooden edifice, the door of which was heavily timbered with oak, and studded with iron spikes.

24. One thing was certain, that the *white* kitten had had nothing to do with it—it was the black kitten's fault entirely.

25. Once upon a time and a very good time it was there was a moocow coming down along the road and this moocow that was coming down along the road met a nicens little boy named baby tuckoo . . .

Titles	**Authors**
The Call of the Wild	Louisa May Alcott
Catch-22	Jane Austen
David Copperfield	Samuel Beckett
The Da Vinci Code	Dan Brown
The Good Earth	Pearl Buck

The Grapes of Wrath	Edward Bulwer-Lytton
Harry Potter and the Sorcerer's Stone	Lewis Carroll
Little Women	Charles Dickens
Lord of the Flies	William Golding
Love Story	Nathaniel Hawthorne
"The Metamorphosis"	Joseph Heller
Moby-Dick	Ernest Hemingway
Native Son	James Joyce
"The Necklace"	Franz Kafka
Nineteen Eighty-Four	Ken Kesey
The Old Man and the Sea	Harper Lee
One Flew Over the Cuckoo's Nest	Jack London
Paul Clifford	Guy de Maupassant
A Portrait of the Artist as a Young Man	Herman Melville
Pride and Prejudice	George Orwell
The Scarlet Letter	J. K. Rowling
Stuart Little	Erich Segal

Through the Looking-Glass	John Steinbeck
To Kill a Mockingbird	E. B. White
Waiting for Godot	Richard Wright

Answers

1. Herman Melville, *Moby-Dick* 2. Samuel Beckett, *Waiting for Godot* 3. Jane Austen, *Pride and Prejudice* 4. George Orwell, *Nineteen Eighty-Four* 5. J. K. Rowling, *Harry Potter and the Sorcerer's Stone*

6. Charles Dickens, *David Copperfield* 7. Pearl Buck, *The Good Earth* 8. Joseph Heller, *Catch-22* 9. John Steinbeck, *The Grapes of Wrath* 10. Guy de Maupassant, "The Necklace"

11. Dan Brown, *The Da Vinci Code* 12. Franz Kafka, "The Metamorphosis" 13. Jack London, *The Call of the Wild* 14. William Golding, *Lord of the Flies* 15. Richard Wright, *Native Son*

16. Harper Lee, *To Kill a Mockingbird* 17. Edward Bulwer-Lytton, *Paul Clifford* 18. Ken Kesey, *One Flew Over the Cuckoo's Nest* 19. Louisa May Alcott, *Little Women* 20. Erich Segal, *Love Story*

21. Ernest Hemingway, *The Old Man and the Sea* 22. E. B. White, *Stuart Little* 23. Nathaniel Hawthorne, *The Scarlet Letter* 24. Lewis Carroll, *Through the Looking-Glass* 25. James Joyce, *A Portrait of the Artist as a Young Man*

Unreal Estate

He wrote under the pseudonyms Schuyler Stanton, Floyd Akers, and Edith Van Dyne, but he is best known as L. Frank Baum. In 1900, he sat down to write a children's book about a girl named Dorothy who was swept away to a fantastic land inhabited by munchkins and witches and a scarecrow, a tin man, and a lion.

The fairy tale began as a bedtime story for Baum's children and their friends and soon spilled over into several evening sessions. During one of the tellings, Baum was asked the name of the strange place to which Dorothy was swept away. Glancing about the room, Baum's eyes fell upon the drawers of a filing cabinet labeled "A–N" and "O–Z."

Noting that the letters on the second label spelled out the *ah*s uttered by his rapt listeners, Baum named his fantastic land Oz. Ever since, *The Wonderful Wizard of Oz* has lived in the hearts of children—and grown-ups.

For many lovers of literature, places that exist only between the covers of books are as vivid as places that actually exist on gas station maps. If you are one of those people for whom Oz is as real as Oslo, Camelot is as real as Camden, and Wonderland is as real as Disneyland, this quiz is for you.

Match each imaginary locale listed in the left-hand column with the name of its creator listed in the right-hand column:

1.	Baskerville Hall	Sherwood Anderson
2.	Belle Reeve	Piers Anthony
3.	Bleak House	Aristophanes
4.	Brideshead	Jane Austen
5.	Cloud Cuckoo Land	James Barrie
6.	Darkover	L. Frank Baum
7.	Dune	Marion Zimmer Bradley
8.	East Egg	Charlotte Brontë

9.	Egdon Heath	Emily Brontë
10.	The Emerald City	John Bunyan
11.	The Forest of Arden	Lewis Carroll
12.	Gopher Prairie	Miguel de Cervantes
13.	Hogwart's School	Samuel Taylor Coleridge
14.	La Mancha	Charles Dickens
15.	Land of the Lotus-Eaters	Sir Arthur Conan Doyle
16.	Lilliput	George Eliot
17.	Looking-Glass House	William Faulkner
18.	Lowood	F. Scott Fitzgerald
19.	Middle Earth	Kenneth Grahame
20.	Middlemarch	Thomas Hardy
21.	Narnia	Frank Herbert
22.	Never-Never-Land	James Hilton
23.	Northanger Abbey	Homer
24.	Oceania	Stephen King
25.	Pandemonium	C. S. Lewis
26.	Pencey Prep	Sinclair Lewis
27.	Pooh Corner	A. A. Milne
28.	The Republic	John Milton
29.	Salem's Lot	Thomas More
30.	Shangri-La	George Orwell

31. The Slough of
    Despond   Plato
32. Starkville   J. K. Rowling
33. Toad Hall   J. D. Salinger
34. Utopia   Sir Walter Scott
35. Waverley Hall   William Shakespeare
36. Winesburg   Jonathan Swift
37. Wuthering Heights   J. R. R. Tolkien
38. Xanadu   Evelyn Waugh
39. Xanth   Edith Wharton
40. Yoknatapawpha
    County   Tennessee Williams

Answers

1. Sir Arthur Conan Doyle 2. Tennessee Williams 3. Charles Dickens 4. Evelyn Waugh 5. Aristophanes 6. Marion Zimmer Bradley 7. Frank Herbert 8. F. Scott Fitzgerald 9. Thomas Hardy 10. L. Frank Baum

11. William Shakespeare 12. Sinclair Lewis 13. J. K. Rowling 14. Miguel de Cervantes 15. Homer 16. Jonathan Swift 17. Lewis Carroll 18. Charlotte Brontë 19. J. R. R. Tolkien 20. George Eliot

21. C. S. Lewis 22. James Barrie 23. Jane Austen 24. George Orwell 25. John Milton 26. J. D. Salinger 27. A. A. Milne 28. Plato 29. Stephen King 30. James Hilton

31. John Bunyan 32. Edith Wharton 33. Kenneth Grahame 34. Thomas More 35. Sir Walter Scott 36. Sherwood Anderson 37. Emily Brontë 38. Samuel Taylor Coleridge 39. Piers Anthony 40. William Faulkner

Super
Sleuths

Sir Arthur Conan Doyle wanted to give his fictional detective an outlandish first name and thought seriously about Sherrinford. Ultimately, the doctor-turned-author settled on the Christian name Sherlock, after a Yorkshire bowler named Mordecai Sherlock, against whom he had played cricket.

After seriously considering the last name of Hope, suggested by a whaling ship named the *Hope,* Doyle chose that of a much-admired American writer of the time, Oliver Wendell Holmes. A distinguished, brilliant, and multitalented pioneer in medicine and criminal psy-

chology, Oliver Wendell was the perfect proto-
type for Doyle's consulting detective. That's why
the world's most famous fictional sleuth isn't
known as Sherrinford Hope.

Dashiell Hammett, on the other hand, gave
his most famous creation his own first name,
which was Sam, as in Samuel Dashiell Hammett.
That's why the classic hard-boiled detective in
The Maltese Falcon isn't Dash Spade.

The word *sleuth* is a clipping of *sleuthhound*,

the Scottish bloodhound noted for its dogged pursuit of game, suspects, or fugitives. Match each author in the left-hand column with his or her sleuth to the right. One author has two sleuths:

Margery Allingham	Roderick Alleyn
Edmund Clerihew Bentley	Lew Archer
Earl Derr Biggers	Father Brown
John Dickson Carr	Albert Campion
Raymond Chandler	Brother Cadfael
Leslie Charteris	Steve Carella
G. K. Chesterton	Charlie Chan
Agatha Christie	Nick and Nora Charles
Edmund Crispin	Sergeant Cribb
Antonia Fraser	Nancy Drew
Emile Gaboriau	C. Auguste Dupin
Erle Stanley Gardner	Dr. Gideon Fell
Sue Grafton	Gervase Fen
Martha Grimes	Alan Grant
Dashiell Hammett	Cordelia Gray
P. D. James	Mike Hammer
Carolyn Keene	Richard Jury
Harry Kemelman	Monsieur Lecoq
Peter Lovesey	Inspector Maigret

John D. MacDonald

Ross MacDonald

Ngaio Marsh

Ed McBain

Sara Paretsky

Ellis Peters

Edgar Allan Poe

Dorothy Sayers

Georges Simenon

Mickey Spillane

Rex Stout

Josephine Tey

S. S. Van Dine

Philip Marlowe

Miss Jane Marple

Perry Mason

Travis McGee

Kinsey Millhone

Hercule Poirot

The Saint
    (Simon Templar)

Jemima Shore

Rabbi David Small

Philip Trent

Philo Vance

V. I. Warshawski

Lord Peter Wimsey

Nero Wolfe

Answers

Margery Allingham—Albert Campion; Edmund Clerihew Bentley—Philip Trent; Earl Derr Biggers—Charlie Chan; John Dickson Carr—Dr. Gideon Fell; Raymond Chandler—Philip Marlowe; Leslie Charteris—The Saint (Simon Templar);

G. K. Chesterton—Father Brown; Agatha Christie—Miss Jane Marple, Hercule Poirot

Edmund Crispin—Gervase Fen; Antonia Fraser—Jemima Shore; Emile Gaboriau—Monsieur Lecoq; Erle Stanley Gardner—Perry Mason; Sue Grafton—Kinsey Millhone; Martha Grimes—Richard Jury; Dashiell Hammett—Nick and Nora Charles; P. D. James—Cordelia Gray

Carolyn Keene—Nancy Drew; Harry Kemelman—Rabbi David Small; Peter Lovesey—Sergeant Cribb; John D. MacDonald—Travis McGee; Ross MacDonald—Lew Archer; Ngaio Marsh—Roderick Alleyn; Ed McBain—Steve Carella; Sara Paretsky—V. I. Warshawski

Ellis Peters—Brother Cadfael; Edgar Allan Poe—C. Auguste Dupin; Dorothy Sayers—Lord Peter Wimsey; Georges Simenon—Inspector Maigret; Mickey Spillane—Mike Hammer; Rex Stout—Nero Wolfe; Josephine Tey—Alan Grant; S. S. Van Dine—Philo Vance

Notable, Quotable Poetry

"There's no money in poetry," quoth the poet laureate Robert Graves, "but there's also no poetry in money." While it is true that rhyme doesn't pay, poets gain a foothold on eternity through their poems, which for some people is even better than money. What follows are some of the most memorable and enduring lines in the mighty line of English poetry. Identify the sources of the following quotations by title and author:

1. Whan that Aprill with his shoures soote
   The droghte of March hath perced to the roote

2. Shall I compare thee to a summer's day?
   Thou art more lovely and more temperate

3. Death be not proud

4. 'Twas brillig, and the slithy toves
   Did gyre and gimble in the wabe:
   All mimsy were the borogoves,
   And the mome raths outgrabe.

5. Drink to me only with thine eyes,
   And I will pledge with mine

6. Listen, my children, and you will hear
   Of the midnight ride of Paul Revere.
   On the eighteenth of April in seventy-five;
   Hardly a man is now alive
   Who remembers that famous day and year.

7. The outlook wasn't brilliant for the
   Mudville nine that day;
   The score stood four to two, with but one
      inning left to play.

8. Gather ye rosebuds while ye may.
   Old Time is still a-flying.

9. Once upon a midnight dreary, while I
      pondered, weak and weary,
   Over many a quaint and curious volume of
      forgotten lore,—

10. But at my back I always hear
    Time's winged chariot hurrying near

11. They also serve who only stand and wait.

12. Know then thyself, presume not God to
        scan;
    The proper study of mankind is man.

13. Should auld acquaintance be forgot,
    And never brought to min'?
    Should auld acquaintance be forgot,
    And days o' auld lang syne?

14. Tiger! Tiger! Burning bright
    In the forest of the night.
    What immortal hand or eye
    Could frame thy fearful symmetry?

15. Water, water everywhere,
    Nor any drop to drink

16. Hope springs eternal in the human breast

17. A thing of beauty is a joy forever.

18. If winter comes, can spring be far behind?

19. Beauty is truth, truth beauty

20. A Book of Verses underneath the Bough,
    A Jug of Wine, a Loaf of Bread—and Thou

21. God's in his heaven—
    All's right with the world.

22. How do I love thee? Let me count the ways

23. A little learning is a dangerous thing.

24. Do not go gentle into that good night.
    Rage, rage against the dying of the light.

25. By the shores of Gitche Gumee
    By the shining Big-Sea-Water

26. Behind him lay the gray Azores,
    Behind the Gates of Hercules;
    Before him not the ghost of shores,
    Before him only shoreless seas.

27. O Captain! My Captain! Our fearful trip is
       done,
    The ship has weathered every rack, the
       prize we sought is won.

28. Because I could not stop for Death,
    He kindly stopped for me—

29. This is the way the world ends
    Not with a bang but a whimper.

30. The fog comes
    On little cat feet.

31. The woods are lovely, dark and deep,
    But I have promises to keep.

32. Out of the night that covers me,
    Black as the Pit from pole to pole,
    I thank whatever gods may be
    For my unconquerable soul.

33. I must down to seas again, to the lonely
    sea and the sky.
    And all I ask is a tall ship and a star to
    steer her by.

34. Theirs not to make reply,
    Theirs not to reason why,
    Theirs but to do and die;
    Into the valley of Death
    Rode the six hundred.

35. An' the Gobble-uns 'at gits you
            Ef you
                    Don't
                            Watch
                                    Out!

Answers

1. The Canterbury Tales, Geoffrey Chaucer 2. Sonnet XVIII, William Shakespeare 3. "Death Be Not Proud," John Donne 4. "Jabberwocky," Lewis Carroll 5. "Song to Celia," Ben Jonson

6. "Paul Revere's Ride," Henry Wadsworth Longfellow 7. "Casey at the Bat," Ernest Lawrence Thayer 8. "To the Virgins, to Make Much of Time," Robert Herrick 9. "The Raven," Edgar Allan Poe 10. "To His Coy Mistress," Andrew Marvell

11. "On His Blindness," John Milton 12. "An Essay on Man," Alexander Pope 13. "Auld Lang Syne," Robert Burns 14. "The Tiger," William Blake 15. "The Rime of the Ancient Mariner," Samuel Taylor Coleridge

16. "An Essay on Man," Alexander Pope 17. *Endymion,* John Keats 18. "Ode to the West Wind," Percy Bysshe Shelley 19. "Ode on a Grecian Urn," John Keats 20.

The Rubáiyát of Omar Khayyam, Edward FitzGerald

21. *Pippa Passes,* Robert Browning 22. *Sonnets from the Portuguese,* Elizabeth Barrett Browning 23. "Essay on Criticism," Alexander Pope 24. "Do Not Go Gentle into That Good Night," Dylan Thomas 25. "The Song of Hiawatha," Henry Wadsworth Longfellow

26. "Columbus," Joaquin Miller 27. "O Captain! My Captain!," Walt Whitman 28. "Because I could not stop for Death," Emily Dickinson 29. "The Hollow Men," T. S. Eliot 30. "Fog," Carl Sandburg

31. "Stopping by Woods on a Snowy Evening," Robert Frost 32. "Invictus," William Ernest Henley 33. "Sea-Fever," John Masefield 34. "The Charge of the Light Brigade," Alfred, Lord Tennyson 35. "Little Orphan Annie," John Whitcomb Riley

Language Throws the Book at Us

When people misuse words in an illiterate but humorous manner, we call the result a *malapropism*. The word echoes the name of Mrs. Malaprop (from the French *mal a propos*, "not appropriate"), a character who first strode the stage in 1775 in Richard Sheridan's comedy *The Rivals*. Mrs. Malaprop was an "old weather-beaten she dragon" who took special pride in her use of the King's English but who unfailingly mangled big words all the same: "Sure, if I reprehend anything in this world it is the use of my oracular tongue, and a nice derangement of epitaphs!" She meant, of course, that if she comprehended anything, it was a nice arrangement of epithets.

In his epic poem *Paradise Lost,* John Milton invented *Pandemonium*—literally "a place for all the demons"—as the name of the home for Satan and his devilish friends. Because the devils were noisy, the meaning of *pandemonium,* now lowercased, has been broadened to mean "uproar and tumult."

A number of words have been literally and literarily born at the tip of a pen, for our language bestows a special kind of life upon people and places that have existed only in books. Fictional creations though they may be, many of these literary creations have assumed a vitality and longevity that pulse just as powerfully as their flesh-and-blood counterparts. The words that derive from these imaginary names can achieve such wide application that they are no longer written with capital letters.

Using the following descriptions, identify the common words that have sprung from the fertile imaginations of our novelists, playwrights, and poets. Also identify the original names of the characters or works whence they spring:

1. The hero of a novel by Miguel de Cervantes engaged himself in endless knightly quests, rescuing damsels he deemed to be in distress and fighting monsters by tilting against windmills. An adjective formed from his name now describes people who are idealistic and chivalrous to an extravagant degree.

2. The name of a blustering giant in Edmund Spenser's Renaissance epic, *The Faerie Queene*, has become a word for a loud-mouthed boaster who is notably short on performance.

3. Another big-talking giant lumbers through the pages of a novel by Francois Rabelais. This giant king was so huge that it took 17,913 cows to provide him with milk and 1,100 hides to make him a pair of shoes. Today an adjective form of his name denotes anything of a colossal scale.

4. In 1516, Sir Thomas More wrote a book about an ideal state. As a name for both the novel and the place, More coined a name from the Greek word parts *ou*, "no," *topos*, "place," and *-ia*, "state of being." The resulting word has come to designate any ideal society.

5. The imagination of Charles Dickens teemed with colorful characters who so embodied particular traits in human nature that their names have come to stand for those qualities. Thus, a fawning toady is often called a *Uriah Heep* and a tyrannical teacher a *Gradgrind*. *Micawberish* has become a synonym for "habitually hopeful" and *Pecksniffery* a noun for religious hypocrisy. These name words have retained their capital letters, but one that is rapidly evolving into lower case began life as a character in *A Christmas Carol*. Even though old Ebenezer's heart turned from stone to gold at the end of the story, we still use his name to describe a mean and miserly person.

Answers

1. Quixotic—Don Quixote
2. Braggadocio—Braggadocio
3. Gargantuan—Gargantua
4. Utopia—*Utopia*
5. Scrooge—Scrooge

All's Well That Ends Well

"L-d, said my mother, what is all this story about?—A COCK and a BULL, said Yorick—And one of the best kind I ever heard" is the sprightly ending of Laurence Sterne's *Tristram Shandy*. Cock and bull stories are so called because ancient fables were filled with birds and animals walking and talking and acting like people.

The problem with stories, be they cock and bull or not, is that they require to be wound up. In that process, some stories go dead, while others conclude memorably. "Great is the art of the beginning, but greater the art is of ending," wrote Thomas Fuller.

From the list that follows, select the titles and name the authors of the literary works, quoted below, that end well:

1. But I reckon I got to light out for the Territory ahead of the rest because Aunt Sally she's going to adopt me and sivilize me and I can't stand it. I been there before.

2. "After all, tomorrow is another day."

3. So we beat on, boats against the current, borne back ceaselessly into the past.

4. Villains! I shrieked, dissemble no more! I admit the deed!—tear up the planks!—here! here!—it is the beating of his hideous heart!

5. They endured.

6. "They don't know we're not allowed to use magic at home. I'm going to have a lot of fun with Dudley this summer. . . ."

7. Don't ever tell anybody anything. If you do, you start missing everybody.

8. It is a far, far better thing that I do, than I have ever done; it is a far, far better rest that I go to, than I have ever known.

9. So I awoke, and behold, it was a dream.

10. I lingered round them, under that benign

sky: watched the moths fluttering among the heath and harebells: listened to the soft wind breathing through the grass; and wondered how any one could ever imagine unquiet slumbers for the sleepers in that quiet earth.

11. That might be the subject of a new story—but our present story is ended.

12. Vale.

13. There were three thousand six hundred and fifty-three days like this in his sentence, from reveille to lights out. The three extra ones were because of the leap years.

14. There is more day to dawn. The sun is but a morning star.

15. Nowadays the world is lit by lightning! Blow out your candles, Laura—and so goodbye . . .

Titles	Authors
The Adventures of Huckleberry Finn	Emily Brontë
The Catcher in the Rye	John Bunyan
Crime and Punishment	Miguel de Cervantes
Don Quixote	Charles Dickens
The Glass Menagerie	Fyodor Dostoevsky
The Great Gatsby	F. Scott Fitzgerald
Gone with the Wind	William Faulkner
Harry Potter and the Sorcerer's Stone	Margaret Mitchell
One Day in the Life of Ivan Denisovich	Edgar Allan Poe
Pilgrim's Progress	J. D. Salinger
The Sound and the Fury	J. K. Rowling
A Tale of Two Cities	Alexandr Solzhenitsyn
"The Tell-Tale Heart"	Henry David Thoreau
Walden	Mark Twain
Wuthering Heights	Tennessee Williams

Answers

1. Mark Twain, *The Adventures of Huckleberry Finn* 2. Margaret Mitchell, *Gone with the Wind* 3. F. Scott Fitzgerald, *The Great Gatsby* 4. Edgar Allan Poe, "The Tell-Tale Heart" 5. William Faulkner, *The Sound and the Fury*

6. J. K. Rowling, *Harry Potter and the Sorcerer's Stone* 7. J. D. Salinger, *The Catcher in the Rye* 8. Charles Dickens, *A Tale of Two Cities* 9. John Bunyan, Part One of *Pilgrim's Progress* 10. Emily Brontë, *Wuthering Heights*

11. Fyodor Dostoevsky, *Crime and Punishment* 12. Miguel de Cervantes, *Don Quixote* 13. Alexandr Solzhenitsyn, *One Day in the Life of Ivan Denisovich* 14. Henry David Thoreau, *Walden* 15. Tennessee Williams, *The Glass Menagerie*